Fill Your BUCKET

Kelly Tanner

THIS BOOK BELONGS TO:

_____

Once upon a time, in a land of monsters and magic,
Lived a creature quite peculiar, his name was Eric.

Eye Land

Scare-Sea

Forest of Fears

Monster Lagoon

He was huge and hairy, with a horn and fangs so sharp,
But despite his appearance, he had a gentle heart.

He had a special bucket that he carried with care,
It was full of happiness, and he took it everywhere.

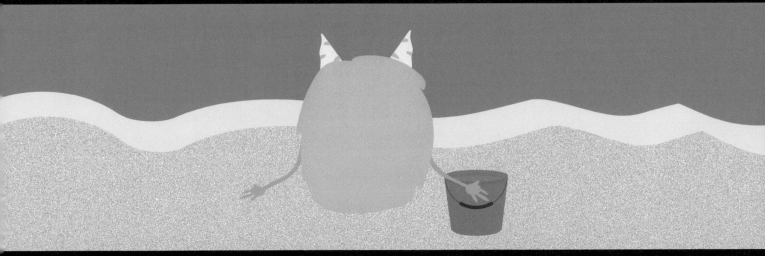

But every now and then, his bucket would run dry,
And Eric would feel anxious and upset... he would even cry.
So, he'd fill it with things, that made him feel glad,
And soon enough, he was no longer sad.

He'd go for a walk in the bright sunshine...

He would read his favourite book...

... Or watch a funny show.
And before he knew it, his happiness would grow.

He'd spend time with his friends, and play games with glee.

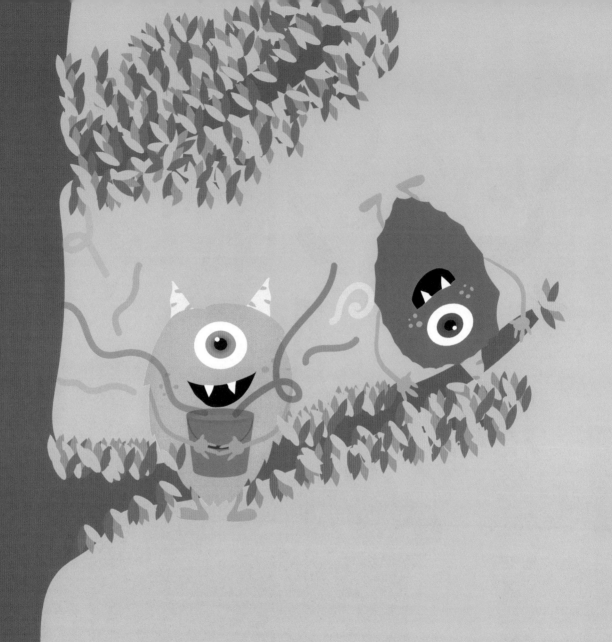

He'd spend time with his sister, climbing the tallest tree!

Sometimes, he'd paint or draw, or sing a sweet tune.

Or take a deep breath and meditate until noon.

He'd do what he loved, and he'd do it with pride,
And soon enough, his bucket was full up inside!

One day, he was walking through the Forest of Fears,
when he stumbled upon a girl whose eyes sparkled with tears.

She was kind and gentle, with a smile that shone bright,
Eric knew right then that he could shed some light.

He gave her some happiness, to fill her bucket anew,
And she replied with love and joy and laughter so true.

From that day on, Eric walked with a skip in his step,
His bucket overflowing, he felt no more regret.
For he had found the key to keep his monster heart so pure,
And he knew that with love and happiness, he could always endure.

So, if you ever feel anxious or sad
Just remember this monster and his bucket of glad.
Fill it with happiness, and things that you love,
And soon enough, your heart will rise above.

How can you fill your bucket?

How can you fill someone's bucket?

The End.

Printed in Great Britain
by Amazon

25133799R00021